My First

FRENCH

BAKERY

BARBARA
BEERY

FAMILIUS

Published by Familius LLC, www.familius.com

Familius books are available at special discounts for bulk purchases for sales promotions
or for family or corporate use. Special editions, including personalized covers, excerpts
of existing books, or books with corporate logos, can be created in large quantities for
special needs. For more information, contact Premium Sales at 559-876-2170 or email
specialmarkets@familius.com.

Library of Congress Catalog-in-Publication Data
2015943233   ISBN 9781942934110

Edited by Laurie Duersch   Photography by Lisette Donado
Cover and book design by David Miles

10 9 8 7 6 5 4 3 2 1   First Edition   Printed in China

RECIPE SKILL LEVEL:

SIMPLE   A BIT HARDER   A BIT CHALLENGING

CONTENTS

· · · · · · · · · · · ·

MY LITTLE MACARONS

· · · · · · · · · · · ·

MES PETITS MACARONS

⁍ *Ingredients* ⁌

MACARONS

1 cup powdered sugar

3/4 cup almond flour

2 large egg whites, room temperature

1/8 teaspoon cream of tartar

1/4 cup superfine sugar

BUTTERCREAM FILLING

3 large egg whites

1 cup sugar

1 cup unsalted butter, at room temperature

Makes 16-18 macarons

MACARONS

1   Preheat the oven to 375°F. Line two baking sheets with parchment paper. Trace 1-inch circles 1 inch apart on the paper to use as a guideline for piping macaron dough. Turn over the marked side of each parchment paper so that no pencil marks get on the macarons. Set aside until ready to use.

2   Pulse powdered sugar and almond flour in a food processor until combined. Sift the mixture thoroughly.

3   Whisk egg whites with a mixer on medium speed until foamy (about 3–4 minutes). Add cream of tartar, and whisk until soft peaks form. Reduce speed to low and add superfine sugar. Increase speed to high, and whisk until stiff peaks form (about 8 minutes).

4   Sift the flour mixture over the whipped egg whites, and fold until mixture is smooth and shiny.

5   Transfer batter to a pastry bag fitted with a 1/2-inch plain round tip, and pipe 1-inch rounds on each designated circle, dragging the pastry tip to the side of each macaron round rather than forming peaks.

6   Tap the bottom of each sheet to release trapped air. Let stand at room temperature for 15 minutes. Reduce oven temperature to 325°F.

7   Bake 1 sheet at a time, rotating the baking sheet halfway through, until macarons are crisp and firm (about 10 minutes). After each batch, increase oven temperature to 375°F, heat for 5 minutes, then reduce to 325°F.

8 Let macarons cool on the sheets for 2–3 minutes and transfer to cool completely on a wire rack. (If macarons stick, spray water underneath parchment on hot sheet. The steam will help release macarons.)

Unfilled macarons can be frozen for up to 3 months in plastic wrap.

Make different flavors of macarons by adding the flavor before adding the flour in the recipe. For fruit flavoring, add 1 tablespoon of fruit jam or preserves and 2 drops of the appropriate paste food color for the fruit chosen. For mint, add 1/4 teaspoon of peppermint extract and 2 drops of green food coloring.

BUTTERCREAM FILLING

1 In the bowl of an electric mixer, whisk egg whites and sugar until combined.

2 Set the mixer bowl over a saucepan of simmering water and heat the mixture, whisking often, until it feels warm to the touch and the sugar is dissolved (about 3–5 minutes).

3 Transfer the bowl to the mixer, and fit it with the whisk attachment. Whip on high speed until mixture is stiff and shiny (about 3–5 minutes).

4 Add butter, one piece at a time, and continue mixing until the butter is thoroughly incorporated.

The filling can be kept, covered and refrigerated, for up to a week. Bring it to room temperature before stirring.

FILL AND ASSEMBLE THE MACARONS

1 Fill a pastry bag with the buttercream and fit the bag with a 1/2-inch round tip, or fill a resealable plastic bag and snip about 1/2 inch off the bottom corner.

2 Pipe a small round in the center of one macaron (1 teaspoon or less) and top with another macaron of similar size. Continue until all the macarons are filled and assembled.

3 For variety, replace the buttercream filling with 1 teaspoon of fruit jam, Nutella, peanut butter, or other filling.

FRENCH VANILLA CUPCAKES

. . . .

PETITS GÂTEAUX À LA VANILLE

⧓ Ingredients ⧓

CUPCAKES

1 box French vanilla cake mix

1/2 cup sugar

1/2 cup water

1/2 cup coconut oil

4 eggs, room temperature

1 cup cream cheese, room temperature

1 tablespoon vanilla extract

1 teaspoon almond extract

BUTTERCREAM ICING

1 cup salted butter

1 teaspoon vanilla extract

3 3/4 cups unsifted powdered sugar

2–4 tablespoons half-and-half

DECORATING

White, turquoise, and pale pink fondant

CUPCAKES

1 Preheat the oven to 325°F. Line two cupcake pans with liners and set aside until ready to use.

2 Place all ingredients in a bowl and mix on low with an electric mixer for 1 minute. Scrape down sides. Increase mixer to medium speed and beat for 1 minute more. The batter should be smooth and thickened.

3 Scoop 1/4 cup batter into each cupcake mold and bake for 20–25 minutes.

4 Remove the cupcakes from the oven and let them cool in pans for 5 minutes. Remove them from pans and let them cool on a rack completely before frosting and decorating.

Makes 24 cupcakes

BUTTERCREAM ICING

1 Cream the butter and vanilla, adding powdered sugar in 1/2-cup increments. Add the half-and-half 2 tablespoons at a time until the desired spreading consistency is reached.

CUPCAKE DECORATING

1 Spread a thin layer of buttercream icing onto each cupcake.

2 When working with fondants, always dust the work surface lightly with cornstarch. Roll out fondants 1/8-inch thick.

3 Use a cutter slightly larger than the circumference of your cupcakes to cut one circle for each cupcake. Place each on top of a frosted cupcake.

4 To make roses, form a small, thin snake about 1 1/2–2 inches long and roll it up, jelly-roll style, to create a rose.

5 Cut out leaves using a small leaf cookie cutter. To make veins in leaves, press in the design with a toothpick.

6 To create dots, lines, or other designs, use more fondant or a piping bag filled with buttercream icing.

MADELEINES

· · · · · · · ·

LA MADELEINE

❧ Ingredients ❧

1 tablespoon butter, softened

2 eggs

1/3 cup granulated sugar

1/4 teaspoon sea salt

1 teaspoon vanilla extract

1/4 teaspoon almond extract

1/2 cup all-purpose flour, sifted

1 teaspoon grated lemon zest

4 tablespoons unsalted butter, melted and cooled

Powdered sugar for dusting

Makes 1 dozen
Madeleines

For extra fun, dip the Madeleines in melted chocolate or candy coating and decorate with colored sprinkles.

1 Preheat the oven to 375°F.

2 Using a pastry brush, heavily brush softened butter over each of the twelve molds in a Madeleine pan, carefully buttering every ridge. Dust the molds with flour, tilting the pan in different directions to coat the surfaces evenly. Turn the pan upside down and tap it gently to dislodge the excess flour.

3 In a large bowl, combine the eggs, granulated sugar, and salt. Using a handheld mixer on medium-high speed, beat the mixture vigorously until pale, thick, and fluffy (about 5 minutes). Beat in the vanilla and almond extracts. Sprinkle the sifted flour over the egg mixture and stir or beat on low speed to incorporate.

4 Gently fold in the lemon zest and the melted butter until evenly mixed.

5 Divide the batter among the prepared molds, using a heaping tablespoon of batter for each mold. Bake the Madeleines until the tops spring back when lightly touched (about 8–12 minutes).

6 Remove the pan from the oven and invert it over a wire rack, then tap it on the rack to release the Madeleines.

7 Let the Madeleines cool on the rack for 10 minutes. Using a fine-mesh sieve, dust the tops with powdered sugar and serve.

PERFECT PETIT FOURS

. . . .

EXCELLENTS PETITS FOURS

⊰ Ingredients ⊱

1 purchased family-size pound cake loaf

POURABLE FONDANT

6 cups powdered sugar

2 tablespoons light corn syrup

1/2 cup water

1 teaspoon no-color almond extract

Gel or paste food coloring, if desired

DECORATIONS

Sprinkles, fresh edible flowers, store-bought sugar decorations

Makes about 16 servings

CAKE

1 Trip 1/4-inch of crust from the top, bottom, and ends of the pound cake. Cut the cake into 1-inch thick slices. Use 1–1 1/2-inch cookie cutters of any shape and cut 2–3 shapes from each slice of pound cake. Place cut-out cakes on a wire rack set over a foil-lined sheet pan.

FONDANT AND DECORATIONS

2 To prepare the fondant, mix the powdered sugar, corn syrup, water, and almond extract together over medium-low heat in a medium saucepan until they are warmed and look smooth and creamy. Remove from heat and cool for about 10 minutes in pan before icing the petit fours.

3 If using food coloring, divide the fondant equally between several small bowls and stir enough food coloring into each one until the desired color is reached. Spoon the fondant over each cake and decorate with sprinkles, flowers, and sugar decorations. Allow them to stand uncovered at room temperature for about 30 minutes or until dry.

4 Carefully lift the cakes from wire rack using an off-set spatula and transfer to a serving platter.

Petits fours may be kept in an airtight container for up to 3 days.

SWEET SUGAR SABLES

· · · · · · · · · · · ·

SABLES SUCRÉS

⅃ Ingredients ⅃

1/2 cup butter, room
temperature

1/2 cup sugar

1 egg yolk

1 teaspoon vanilla extract

1 cup unbleached all-purpose
flour

1/4 teaspoon salt

1 egg, beaten

Sanding sugar*

Makes about 2
dozen sables

These little sugary
cookies are delicious and
colorful with a dollop of
your favorite jam.

1 Cream the butter and sugar. Add the egg yolk and
vanilla and beat thoroughly. In another bowl, whisk
together the flour and salt. Add that to the butter
mixture and blend until the dough is smooth.

2 On a lightly floured surface, roll the dough into
cylinders about 1–2 inches in diameter. Wrap in
waxed paper or plastic wrap and chill for at least an
hour.

3 Preheat oven to 350°F. Line a baking sheet with
parchment paper and set aside until ready to use.
Remove logs from fridge and brush with beaten egg
and roll in sugar.

4 With a sharp knife, slice the dough into rounds
about 1/3-inch thick.

5 Place dough rounds 1 inch apart on the prepared
baking sheet and bake for about 10 minutes or
until the cookies are light golden brown around the
edges.

6 Remove from the oven and cool on baking sheet for
10 minutes before removing and cooling completely
on a wire rack.

*Sanding sugar has much larger grains than
granulated sugar. It is often used by pastry chefs to
garnish cookies that are not iced.

FRENCH CHOCOLATE CAKE

· · · · · · · · · · · ·

FONDANT AU CHOCOLAT

❧ Ingredients ❧

1 tablespoon butter, melted

1 cup milk chocolate or semi-sweet chocolate chips

1 cup butter, room temperature

6 eggs, room temperature

1 1/4 cups sugar

1/8 teaspoon of sea salt

1 cup all-purpose flour

Makes 1
dozen cakes

1 Preheat the oven to 350°F. Use a pastry brush to thoroughly coat the insides of eight small baking dishes (ramekins) or silicone baking molds with a little melted butter. Set aside until ready to use.

2 Place the chocolate chips and 1 cup butter in a microwave-safe bowl. Microwave for 30 seconds and stir. If not completely melted, heat for another 15 seconds.

3 In another bowl, mix the eggs, sugar, and salt with a whisk until creamy and pale yellow in color. Pour the melted chocolate into the egg mixture and whisk until well combined, then add the flour. Whisk again well until all ingredients are combined. The batter will be thin.

4 Pour the batter into the ramekins and bake for 10 to 12 minutes. Remove from oven and allow to cool 10–15 minutes before serving.

This recipe can be made ahead of time. Place in dishes and refrigerate the batter to bake later in the day. Just remove from the fridge and allow to come to room temperature before baking.

LITTLE CUTIE FRENCH CLAFOUTI

· · · · · · · · · · · · ·

CLAFOUTIS

⤜ Ingredients ⤛

1 cup whole milk

3 eggs

1/2 cup sugar

1 teaspoon vanilla extract

2 tablespoons butter, melted

1/2 cup all-purpose flour

2 cups of fruit topping (cherries, raspberries, or strawberries)

Powdered sugar, for garnish

1 Preheat the oven to 325°F.

2 In a large bowl, whisk together the milk, eggs, sugar, vanilla, and butter until the sugar is dissolved. Add the flour and whisk until smooth. Pour the batter into a cast-iron skillet, a pie pan, individual pans, or ramekins.

3 Top with your favorite fruit or flavorings.

4 Bake until the clafoutis are puffed and light golden brown (about 35–40 minutes). Serve immediately with a dusting of powdered sugar.

Makes 8 individual clafoutis or 1 ten-inch claflouti

TASTY FRUIT TARTS

· · · · · · · · · · · ·

TARTES AUX FRUITS

Ingredients

SWEET PASTRY DOUGH

2 1/2 cups all-purpose flour

3 tablespoons sugar

1 cup unsalted butter, chilled and cut into small pieces

2 large egg yolks

1/4 cup ice water

PASTRY CREAM

4 large egg yolks

1/2 cup sugar

1/4 cup cornstarch

1/4 teaspoon kosher salt

1 1/2 cups whole milk

1 teaspoon pure vanilla extract

4 tablespoons unsalted butter, cut into small pieces

Assorted fresh seasonal fruits

Makes 8 individual tarts

SWEET PASTRY DOUGH

1 In the bowl of a food processor, combine the flour and sugar. Add the butter and process until the mixture resembles coarse meal.

2 In a separate small bowl, lightly beat the egg yolks and add the ice water.

3 With the food processor running, add the egg/water mixture in a slow, steady stream through the feed tube. Pulse until the dough holds together without being wet or sticky. If the dough is too dry, add more ice water, 1 tablespoon at a time.

4 Divide the dough into two equal balls and flatten each into a disc. Wrap them in plastic and place them in the refrigerator to chill for 1 hour or longer.

5 Remove the dough from the refrigerator and, on a lightly floured work surface, roll it out to about 1/4-inch thick.

6 Using the individual tart pans as you would a cookie cutter, cut out the dough for each pan.

7 Lightly push the dough into each tart pan with your index finger. Use your fingers to press the edges and tear off excess dough.

8 Place the tart shells on a baking sheet and chill uncovered in the refrigerator until firm (about 30 minutes).

9 Preheat the oven to 375°F. Remove the tarts from the fridge and prick the bottom of the dough all over with a fork.

10 Depending on the size of your tart shells, bake for 8–10 minutes or until light golden brown.

11 Remove from the oven and cool for 2–3 minutes before removing from tart pans.

PASTRY CREAM

1 In a medium saucepan, whisk together the egg yolks, sugar, cornstarch, and salt.

2 Whisk in the milk. Cook over medium-high heat, whisking constantly, until the mixture has thickened to the consistency of creamy salad dressing (about 2–4 minutes).

3 Remove from heat and whisk in the vanilla. Then add the butter, a few pieces at a time, until melted and smooth.

4 Pour the cream into a bowl. Place a piece of parchment or wax paper directly on the surface of the pastry cream and refrigerate it until completely cool, at least 2 hours and up to 2 days.

ASSEMBLE THE TARTS

1 Spoon pastry cream into each tart shell, almost up to the top of the pastry crust. Top with assorted fruits and serve immediately, or store in the refrigerator uncovered for up to 5 hours.

In a hurry? Try these shortcuts: Substitute refrigerated pie crust dough for the sweet pastry dough and substitute a rich, thick lemon or vanilla yogurt like Noosa® for the pastry cream.

CREAM PUFFS

· · · · · · · ·

CHOUX À LA CRÈME

ঽ *Ingredients* ঽ

PASTRY

1/2 cup all-purpose flour

1/2 teaspoon granulated sugar

1/4 teaspoon salt

4 tablespoons unsalted butter, cut into pieces

1/2 cup water

2 large eggs

Powdered sugar, for garnish

VANILLA CHANTILLY CREAM

2 cups heavy whipping cream

2 teaspoons vanilla extract

2 tablespoons (or more) sugar, to taste

Makes 1 dozen puffs

PASTRY

1 Preheat the oven to 400°F and place the rack in the center of the oven. Line a baking sheet with parchment paper and set it aside until ready to use.

2 In a bowl, sift or whisk together the flour, sugar, and salt.

3 Place the butter and water in a heavy saucepan over medium heat until the butter is completely melted. Add the flour mixture all at once and cook, stirring vigorously until the mixture is smooth and forms a soft ball.

4 Remove from heat and cool for 5 minutes. Add eggs one at a time, beating well after each is added. The mixture should form a smooth paste.

5 Spoon or pipe 12 small mounds of dough onto the prepared baking sheet, spacing about 2 inches apart.

6 Bake for 15 minutes. Then reduce oven temperature to 350°F and continue to bake for another 30–35 minutes, or until the shells are a light golden brown.

7 Turn the oven off. Leave the puffs on the baking sheet in the oven and poke a couple of small holes into each puff with a wooden skewer to allow steam to escape. Leave the oven door slightly open to allow the shells to completely cool and dry out (about 30 minutes).

VANILLA CHANTILLY CREAM

1 Chill the whipping cream, bowl, and beaters in the freezer for 5–10 minutes before whipping the cream (this helps the cream whip faster and fluffier).

2 Remove the cream, bowl, and beaters from freezer and beat the heavy cream, vanilla extract, and sugar together on high speed until soft peaks form.

ASSEMBLY

1 After puffs have cooled completely, fill each with Vanilla Chantilly Cream and dust with powdered sugar.

This Vanilla Chantilly Cream recipe is essential to every French kitchen. Rich whipped cream infused with vanilla extract is a classic embellishment to any French pastry.

You can also fill the puffs with your favorite flavor of ice cream. It's delicious!

Petits pains roulés à la canelle

CHOCOLATE CINNAMON ROLLS

. . . .

PETITS PAINS ROULÉS À LA CANELLE

⸎ Ingredients ⸎

CINNAMON ROLL

1/4 cup white sugar

1/4 cup brown sugar

1 tablespoon cinnamon

2 sheets store-bought frozen puff pastry, thawed but cold

2 tablespoons melted, unsalted butter, cooled

1/2 cup dark chocolate chips

GLAZE

1 cup powdered sugar

2 tablespoons crème fraîche

2 tablespoon half-and-half

Makes
12 rolls

CINNAMON ROLL

1 Preheat the oven to 400°F. Spray a 12-cup muffin pan with non-stick cooking spray. Set aside until ready to use.

2 In a small bowl, combine the two sugars and cinnamon.

3 Slightly roll out both sheets of puff pastry into two identical squares. Brush the pastry all over with the cooled melted butter.

4 Scatter half the cinnamon sugar all over one puff pastry square, and the other half all over the other. Do the same with the chocolate chips.

5 Roll the sweetened puff pastry squares up into logs, as if you were making a jelly roll. Using a serrated knife, trim just the edges off the sides of the logs. Cut each log into 6 equal sized rolls.

6 In each muffin cup, place 1 cinnamon roll, swirl-side up. Bake for 25–30 minutes or until light golden brown. Remove the rolls from the oven and allow to cool slightly before transferring to a serving plate.

GLAZE

1 While rolls are baking, prepare the glaze. Whisk together powdered sugar, crème fraîche, and half-and-half in a bowl until smooth.

2 Drizzle the glaze over warm cinnamon rolls and serve.

The glaze can be made up to 48 hours in advance. Cover and refrigerate until ready to use. This can be reheated in a microwave or over hot water.

MERINGUES

· · · · · · · ·

LES MERINGUES

ৡ Ingredients ৡ

4 egg whites, room temperature

1/4 teaspoon cream of tartar

1 cup superfine sugar

Optional paste food coloring

Makes 18–24
meringues

1 Preheat the oven to 250°F. Line two cookie sheets with foil. Set aside until ready to use.

2 In a large bowl, whip the egg whites with an electric mixer until soft peaks form. Add the cream of tartar. Continue beating and very slowly add the sugar, 1 tablespoon at a time. Continue beating on high until glossy stiff peaks form. Add optional food coloring and blend to incorporate color.

3 Drop well-rounded teaspoons, or use a pastry bag fitted with star or round tip, onto prepared baking sheets.

4 Bake for 90 minutes. Turn off the oven and leave the door closed for another hour for the meringues to cool and dry out.

5 Remove the meringues from the oven and from the baking sheets and store them in an airtight container until ready to use.

MY FIRST YOGURT CAKE

· · · · · · · · · · ·

MON PREMIER GÂTEAU AU YAOURT

Ingredients

1 1/2 cups all-purpose flour

2 teaspoons baking powder

1/8 teaspoon sea salt

Zest from 1 lemon

1 teaspoon lemon juice

1 cup sugar

1/2 cup plain whole-milk yogurt

3 eggs

1/2 cup extra virgin olive oil

1/2 cup chocolate chips or seasonal fresh fruit (optional)

Makes 1
9x5-inch
loaf

1 Preheat the oven to 350°F. Spray the inside of a loaf pan with cooking spray and set aside until ready to use.

2 Whisk the flour, baking powder, and salt together in a bowl.

3 In another bowl, mix the lemon zest and juice into the sugar. Whisk in the yogurt, then the eggs.

4 Gently whisk in the flour mixture. Switch to a spatula and fold in the olive oil. Fold in optional chocolate chips or fresh fruit.

5 Pour contents into the prepared loaf pan, smoothing out the top, and bake for 45–55 minutes or until the top is golden brown and a toothpick inserted in the center comes out clean.

6 Cool in the pan for 5 minutes, then transfer the cake to a rack to cool completely.

May be stored in an airtight container for up to 3 days.

This is the first cake recipe that most French children are taught, due to the easy directions that include using the empty yogurt container to measure out the other ingredients.

CROQUEMBOUCHE

· · · · · · ·

LE CROQUEMBOUCHE

⸲ Ingredients ⸳

75–80 glazed donut holes

1 pound vanilla candy coating

Sprinkles

1 18-inch Styrofoam cone, covered in parchment paper

Toothpicks

Fresh flowers

Serves 20

1 Line two baking sheets with parchment paper. Place the donut holes on each sheet. Set aside until ready to use.

2 Melt the candy coating according to the package directions. Drizzle the candy coating over all of the donut holes and decorate with sprinkles. Place in the refrigerator for 15 minutes to chill.

3 Remove donut holes from the fridge.

4 Arrange one ring of donut holes around the base of the cone, placing them as close together as possible. To attach the donut holes to the cone, push a toothpick all the way through each donut hole until the end goes into the cone. Leave the other end of the toothpick sticking out for now.

5 Attach a second ring of donut holes above the first, again packing them tightly and staggering the placement so the donut holes in the second ring fill in the space and are not directly above donut holes in the first ring.

6 Continue in the same manner, attaching the remaining donut holes until the cone is covered, and place the last donut hole on the top of the cone.

7 Use a thimble or small butter knife to push the protruding toothpick ends into the donut holes so that they are not seen.

FRESH FRUIT GALLETTES

. . . .

GALETTES DE FRUITS FRAIS

⁂ Ingredients ⁂

1 purchased refrigerated pie crust or Sweet Pastry Dough (see page 20)

3 cups fresh seasonal fruits

Pinch of sea salt

Juice and grated zest of 1/2 lemon

3–4 tablespoons cornstarch

1/2 cup sugar

1 egg

2–3 tablespoons cream

Makes 1
gallette

1 Preheat the oven to 400°F. Line a baking pan with parchment paper.

2 Roll out the dough onto the lined baking sheet and place in the fridge while preparing the filling.

3 In a bowl, toss together the fruit, salt, lemon juice and zest, cornstarch, and all but a tablespoon of sugar. Use more cornstarch for juicy stone fruits (like plums, nectarines, or peaches) and less for fruit like blueberries, raspberries, and strawberries.

4 Pile the fruit mixture on the dough circle, leaving a 1 1/2-inch border. Gently fold the border over the edge of the fruit mixture, pleating to hold.

5 Mix egg and cream in a small bowl and whisk to combine. Brush pastry generously with egg and cream mixture. Sprinkle the remaining tablespoon of sugar on the crust.

6 Bake for 35–45 minutes, until the filling bubbles up vigorously and the crust is golden brown. Remove from the oven and cool on the baking pan for 15–20 minutes on a wire rack. Slide it off of the baking pan and serve warm or at room temperature.

VERY GOOD SUGAR COOKIES

· · · · · · · · · · · ·

BISCUITS TRÈS BONS AU SUCRE

⸙ Ingredients ⸙

1/2 cup butter, softened

3/4 cup granulated sugar

1 egg

1 teaspoon vanilla extract

2 cups all-purpose flour

1/2 teaspoon baking soda

1/4 teaspoon salt

Makes 15–18 cookies

1 Preheat the oven to 375°F. Cream the butter in a large mixing bowl. Add the sugar, beating until light and fluffy. Add the egg and vanilla, mixing well.

2 In a separate bowl, combine the flour, baking soda, and salt. Add this to the creamed mixture, blending well. The dough will be very stiff.

3 Divide the dough into thirds. Roll each portion to 1/4-inch thickness on a lightly floured work area. Cut with cookie cutters. Place the cookies 2 inches apart on cookie sheets sprayed with non-stick cooking spray.

4 Bake for 8–10 minutes or until lightly browned. Move the cookies to wire racks to cool completely. Frost and decorate.

CRUSTY FRENCH BAGUETTE

· · · · · · · · · · · ·

BAGUETTE FRANÇAISE CROQUANTE

 **Ingredients**

2 cups very warm water

1 packet yeast

2 tablespoons sugar

1 1/2 teaspoons sea salt

3–4 cups all-purpose flour

Makes 4
baguettes

1 Line a baking sheet with parchment paper and set aside until ready to use.

2 In a large bowl, whisk together the warm water, yeast, and sugar. Set in a draft-free place (inside an oven or microwave works great) for 15 minutes.

3 After 15 minutes, stir in the salt and add the flour a half-cup at a time until the dough becomes soft but not sticky. Knead the dough in the bowl until loose dough balls form.

4 Remove the dough from the bowl and place on floured surface and sprinkle a little flour on top. Cut the dough into four even pieces and roll into four baguettes (long, narrow loaves). Transfer the baguettes to the prepared baking sheet. Snip the top of each loaf with kitchen scissors and allow to rise 30 minutes.

5 Preheat the oven to 425°F while the dough is rising and fill a large ovenproof container with 3–4 cups of ice.

6 Place the baguettes in the oven and set the container of ice on the rack underneath.

7 Do not open your oven for 15 minutes. Bake until golden brown or 15–18 minutes.

8 Remove the baguettes from the oven and the baking sheet and allow to cool on a wire rack for 30 minutes before cutting.

FANCY FRENCH PIZZA

· · · · · · · · · · · ·

PIZZA FRANÇAIS EXTRAVAGANT

❧ Ingredients ❧

1 soft French bread loaf, sliced in half lengthwise

3 tablespoons butter

3 tablespoons extra virgin olive oil

4 cloves of garlic, finely minced

1/8 teaspoon red pepper flakes

1/2 teaspoon dried oregano

1/4 cup fresh parsley and basil, minced and combined

1/2 cup marinara sauce

1 cup shredded mozzarella cheese

Sea salt and freshly ground pepper, to taste

2 tablespoons freshly grated Parmesan cheese

1 Preheat the oven to 400°F. Line a baking sheet with parchment paper and set aside until ready to use.

2 Heat the butter and olive oil in a medium saucepan over low heat until the butter is melted. Add garlic, pepper flakes, and oregano and cook, stirring occasionally, until the garlic is softened but not browned (about 2 minutes). Stir in half the parsley and basil and a big pinch of sea salt.

3 Brush the cut side of each loaf with the herb-butter blend and top with 1/2 cup mozzarella cheese. Place on the prepared baking sheet and bake until cheese is barely melted (about 6–8 minutes).

4 Remove from oven and spread with marinara sauce and sprinkle with the remaining mozzarella. Season with salt and pepper and bake for an additional for 10–12 minutes or until the cheese is melted and the bread is heated through.

5 Remove from the oven and sprinkle with Parmesan cheese and the remaining parsley and basil.

Makes 4–6 servings

QUICHE LORRAINE

....

QUICHE LORRAINE

❧ *Ingredients* ❧

2 purchased refrigerated pie crusts, uncooked

1/2 cup heavy cream

1/2 cup milk

3 eggs

1 tablespoon unsalted butter, melted

1/2 cup grated Gruyère cheese

Sea salt and freshly ground black pepper, to taste

Cayenne pepper, to taste

Freshly grated nutmeg, to taste

3 cooked bacon slices, chopped

Makes 6
4-inch quiches

1 Preheat the oven to 425°F

2 Divide each pie crust into three pieces (six pieces total) and roll each into a ball. Lightly dust your work area with flour and roll out each ball into a 6-inch round.

3 Press each round into a 4-inch quiche pan and fold in the overhang. Press to make the sides thicker than the bottom. Using a fork, prick the dough in several places. Freeze the shells for 15 minutes.

4 Remove from freezer and line the shells with parchment paper. To blind bake, fill each shell with dried beans or pie weights. Place them on a baking sheet and bake for 10 minutes.

5 Remove the parchment and weights and continue baking until the shells are just golden (about 7–10 minutes). Transfer them to a wire rack and cool. Reduce the oven's heat to 375°F.

6 In a bowl, whisk together the cream, milk, eggs, butter, cheese, salt, black pepper, cayenne, and nutmeg. Divide the bacon among the tart shells, then pour the filling into the shells. Bake at 375°F until the filling is set and puffed and the crust is golden brown (about 15–20 minutes). Let it cool for 5 minutes before serving.

Blind baking is sometimes called pre-baking and is the method of baking a pie crust without the filling. Blind baking is necessary to keep pie crust from becoming soggy due to a wet filling, such as a quiche filling.

CROQUE MADAME MUFFINS

· · · · · · · · · · · ·

PETITS CROQUE-MADAMES

⅔ *Ingredients* ⅗

1 tablespoon butter

1 tablespoon all-purpose flour

3/4 cup lukewarm milk

1/2 teaspoon Dijon mustard

1/2 teaspoon nutmeg

1/4 cup grated Gruyère cheese

Sea salt and freshly ground black pepper, to taste

6 large slices of white bread, no crusts, flattened with a rolling pin

3 tablespoons butter, melted

1/4 cup cubed ham

6 large eggs

Makes 6 muffins

1 Melt the butter in a saucepan over medium heat. Add the flour and mix until you have a smooth paste.

2 Remove the saucepan from heat and allow it to cool for a few minutes. Slowly add the milk, whisking constantly. Place the pan back over medium heat, add the mustard and nutmeg, and simmer gently for 5 minutes, whisking often. Once the sauce has thickened, remove it from heat and stir in the cheese. Add salt and pepper to taste.

3 Preheat the oven to 350°F. Spray six extra-large muffin cups lightly with cooking oil. Set aside until ready to use.

4 Brush both sides of each bread slice with melted butter. Press each slice into a muffin cup.

5 Divide the ham equally between the muffin cups and break an egg into each one.

6 Put 2 tablespoons cheese sauce on top of each egg and sprinkle with a little grated Gruyère cheese.

7 Bake for 15 minutes (a slightly longer baking time is needed for a more solid yolk) and serve immediately.

PISTOU SOUP

· · · · · · · · · · · ·

SOUPE AU PISTOU

❧ Ingredients ❧

PISTOU

4 cups packed basil

1 cup grated Parmesan cheese

1/4 cup extra virgin olive oil

1 teaspoon sea salt

2 cloves of garlic, chopped

1 plum tomato, chopped

SOUP

1/4 cup extra virgin olive oil

5 cloves of garlic, finely chopped

3 medium carrots, peeled and finely chopped

2 ribs celery, finely chopped

1 yellow onion, finely chopped

1/2 medium zucchini, chopped

1/4 head Savoy cabbage, cored and thinly shredded

8 cups chicken stock

1 can (15 ounces) chopped tomatoes

1/3 cup broken dried spaghetti

1 can (15 ounces) cannellini beans, rinsed and drained

Sea salt and freshly ground black pepper, to taste

PISTOU

1 Process all Pistou ingredients until finely ground. Empty the mixture into a bowl and season with salt and pepper. Set aside until ready to use.

SOUP

1 Heat oil in a 6-quart saucepan over medium-high heat. Add the garlic, carrots, celery, and onions. Reduce the heat to medium; cook, covered and stirring occasionally, until crisp-tender (about 12–15 minutes).

2 Add the zucchini and cabbage and cook, covered, until wilted (about 3–5 minutes).

3 Add the stock and tomatoes, and bring to a boil. Add the pasta and cook until al dente (about 8 minutes).

4 Mash half the beans with a fork; add to soup along with whole beans. Cook until warmed through.

5 Season with salt and pepper. Ladle the soup into bowls and serve each with a dollop of Pistou.

Pistou is the French word for the Italian word *pesto*.

Makes 8–10 servings

CLASSIC CHEESE FONDUE

. . . .

FONDUE AU FROMAGE CLASSIQUE

⅃ Ingredients ℰ

1 1/2 cups Gruyère cheese, shredded

1 1/2 cups Emmentaler cheese, shredded

2 tablespoons cornstarch

1 clove of garlic, peeled

1/2 cup white grape juice

1/2 cup water

1 teaspoon white wine vinegar

Juice of 1/2 lemon

1/8 teaspoon nutmeg

Sea salt and pepper, to taste

Makes 6 servings

1 Combine the cheeses in a bowl and toss with cornstarch. Lightly smash the clove of garlic and rub it around the inside of a medium sauce pan.

2 Add the grape juice, water, and vinegar to the sauce pan and bring the mixture to a low simmer. Do not boil. Slowly stir in the cheese, 1/4 cup at a time, to ensure a creamy, smooth texture. When all the cheese has been added and the fondue is creamy, stir in the lemon juice, nutmeg, salt, and pepper.

3 Serve warm with your favorite dippers.

Try these fantastic fondue dippers:

- Cherry tomatoes
- Sweet bell peppers
- Apples, such as Granny Smith, or pears, sliced
- Fresh strawberries or dates
- Cubed crusty French bread
- Boiled baby new potatoes in their skins
- Steamed carrots
- Lightly steamed broccoli florets or cauliflower florets
- Lightly steamed asparagus or green beans
- Baby Portobello mushrooms

PROVENÇAL WHITE BEAN DIP

WITH VEGETABLE CRUDITÉS

❧ *Ingredients* ❧

CRUDITÉS

4 rainbow carrots, halved and quartered

1 pint cherry or grape tomatoes

1 large English cucumber, cut into wedges

Snap peas or green beans

8 breakfast radishes, halved lengthwise

1 sweet yellow pepper, sliced

1/2 cup Kalamata olives

WHITE BEAN DIP

1 can (15 ounces) cannellini beans, drained and rinsed

1 clove of garlic

1 teaspoon lemon juice

2 tablespoons olive oil

1 teaspoon dried herbes du Provence

1 Add all the dip ingredients to a food processor and puree until smooth.

2 Spoon equal amounts of dip into 8 cups and serve with assorted veggie dippers.

Makes 8 servings

CHOCOLATE MOUSSE

· · · · · · · · · · · ·

MOUSSE AU CHOCOLAT

ᔅ *Ingredients* ᔒ

3/4 cup water

1 cup high quality chocolate

Ice cubes

Vanilla Chantilly Cream (see page 25), optional

Makes 4
servings

1 Pour water into a saucepan. Heat over medium-low heat and whisk in the chocolate. The result is a smooth but watery sauce.

2 Remove the saucepan from the heat and pour the sauce into a bowl. Place that bowl in a larger bowl of ice. Whisk the chocolate sauce, either manually with a whisk or with an electric mixer (if using an electric mixer, watch closely—it will thicken faster). Whisking creates large air bubbles in the sauce, which makes it thicken.

3 Pour or spoon the mousse into small bowls or jars and serve immediately, or completely cool in the fridge for 1 hour or until ready to serve.

4 Top with Vanilla Chantilly Cream, if desired.

CRÈME BRÛLÉE
········
CRÈME BRÛLÉE

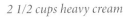 Ingredients

2 1/2 cups heavy cream

4 large egg yolks

1/3 cup granulated sugar, plus
6 teaspoons for topping

1 tablespoon vanilla extract

Makes 6
servings

1 Adjust an oven rack to middle position and preheat the oven to 300°F. Add the heavy cream to a 2-quart saucepan and heat over medium-high heat, stirring frequently until little bubbles form around the sides of the cream.

2 Combine the egg yolks and 1/3 cup of sugar in the bowl of a stand mixer fitted with a whisk attachment. Whisk on medium speed until the mixture is pale yellow and and yolks fall off whisk in ribbons (about 2 minutes), scraping the bowl as necessary. With the mixer running on medium-low speed, slowly add the hot cream mixture. Add the vanilla and whisk until combined.

3 Place a folded kitchen towel (or a few paper towels) on the bottom of a glass baking dish (large enough to hold 6 6-ounce ramekins). Place the ramekins on top of towel and ladle the custard base evenly between them.

4 Remove one ramekin and carefully pour the hot water into the baking dish until it comes halfway up the sides of ramekins. Replace the missing ramekin.

5 Bake until the custard is set but still jiggles in the center (about 40 minutes).

6 Remove the ramekins from the oven and allow them to cool to room temperature without removing ramekins from the water bath. Once cool, remove the ramekins, cover them in plastic wrap, and refrigerate them until set (at least 4 hours or up to 24 hours).

7 To serve, sprinkle each ramekin with 1 teaspoon sugar. Brown with a kitchen torch and serve immediately.

J'ADORE CRÊPES

....

J'ADORE CRÊPES

⸎ Ingredients ⸎

CRÊPES

3/4 cup cold milk

3/4 cup cold water

3 egg yolks

1 tablespoon granulated sugar

1 cup flour

5 tablespoons melted butter

Makes 24 crêpes

Crêpes are paper-thin pancakes that are fun to make, taste great, and always make what's inside of them seem more special. You can roll them, fold them, or layer them—and best of all, you can freeze them. Once defrosted, crêpes are once again soft and delicious.

CRÊPES

1 Place the ingredients in a blender jar in the order in which they are listed. Cover and blend at top speed for 1 minute. Cover and refrigerate for at least 2 hours or overnight.

2 Place 1 teaspoon of room-temperature butter on a paper towel to lightly coat the inside of a crêpe pan or a 6 1/2–7-inch non-stick skillet. Keep paper towels on hand while preparing crêpes, in case you want to give it another wipe.

3 Pour about 1/4 cup batter into the pan and quickly move the pan around in a circular motion so that batter spreads evenly, covering the whole surface with a thin layer.

4 Cook for 1–2 minutes. Then flip the batter to the other side with a metal spatula or with your fingers and cook for about 30 seconds.

5 Slide the crêpes onto a cooling rack and cool several minutes before stacking on a plate.

FILLING

1 Fill your crêpes with your favorite filling and sprinkle with powdered sugar. Some delicious filling possibilities include:

- *Nutella*
- *Fresh fruits of choice, such as strawberries, blueberries, and bananas*
- *Peanut butter or SunButter*
- *Lemon Curd Crème Chantilly*
- *Fruit jam*

BAKED SNOWBALLS

· · · · · · · · · · · ·

BOULES DE NEIGE

⚘ *Ingredients* ⚘

4–6 slices of cake, any kind

Ice cream, frozen yogurt, or sorbet (your favorite flavor)

3 egg whites, room temperature

1/4 teaspoon cream of tartar

4 tablespoons sugar

1 teaspoon vanilla extract

Chocolate syrup, maraschino cherries, sprinkles (for garnish, optional)

Makes 4–6 servings

1 Use 2-inch or 3-inch round baking dishes or ramekins.

2 Cut each slice of cake into a circle so that it fits into the bottom of the baking dish. Place circles of cake on the bottom of each dish.

3 Fill the dishes to the top with ice cream, frozen yogurt, or sorbet. Place the filled dishes on a cookie sheet and put in freezer.

4 Place the egg whites in a mixing bowl and whip until frothy (like soapsuds). Add the cream of tartar and beat until soft peaks form (like shaving cream). While still mixing, gradually add the sugar 1 tablespoon at a time, and then add the vanilla. Continue to beat until the mixture is smooth and shiny (about 2–3 minutes).

5 Preheat the oven to 500°F.

6 Remove ice cream-filled dishes from freezer and spread the "snow" (meringue) over the top of each of the ice cream cups. Make very sure the snow forms a "blanket" over the ice cream. There should be absolutely no ice cream showing.

7 Place the snowballs on a baking sheet in the oven for 1–3 minutes. Watch very closely, as they brown quickly. Remove from the oven and serve immediately. If desired, top with chocolate syrup, maraschino cherries, or sprinkles.

PARISIAN HOT CHOCOLATE

· · · · · · · · · · · ·

CHOCOLAT CHAUD PARISIEN

⸓ Ingredients ⸓

1 1/2 cups whole milk

1/2 cup heavy cream

2 teaspoons powdered sugar

1 cup high-quality chocolate, chopped

Makes 2 servings

1 In a medium saucepan over medium heat, whisk together the whole milk, heavy cream, and powdered sugar until small bubbles appear around the edges. Do not allow the mixture to boil.

2 Remove the saucepan from heat and stir in the chopped chocolate until melted, returning the sauce to low heat if needed for the chocolate to melt completely.

3 Pour into mugs and top with marshmallows or Vanilla Chantilly Cream (see page 25).

SPARKLING FRENCH LEMONADES

· · · · · · · · · · ·

CITRON PRESSÉ

ཉ Ingredients ཉ

1 cup sugar

Peel from 1 lemon, julienned

1 cup water

Juice of 3–4 lemons

2 (1-liter) bottles of sparkling water

Additional sliced lemons and mint or rosemary, for garnish

Makes 10 servings

1 To make lemon syrup, put the sugar, lemon peel, and water in a saucepan. Heat and bring to a boil for 5 minutes.

2 Remove from the heat and pour into a glass jar. Store in the refrigerator to cool. It should be good for up to 1 week.

3 In a large container, combine the cooled lemon syrup, lemon juice, and sparkling water. Add plenty of ice and serve with optional sliced lemons and a mint or rosemary sprig garnish.

Make Different Flavors of French Lemonade:

- **Pink Citrus Lemonade:** Add 2 tablespoons grenadine syrup

- **Blood Orange Lemonade:** Substitute 1 or 2 blood oranges for the lemons

- **Pomegranate-Blueberry Lemonade:** Add 1 tablespoon grenadine syrup and 1 cup frozen blueberries

MEET BARBARA

Barbara Beery, the bestselling author of *The Pink Princess Cookbook*, has been a spokesperson for such national companies as Sun-Maid Raisin, Uncle Ben's, Borden's, Kellogg's Rice Krispies, and Step 2. Barbara has been a contributing writer to *FamilyFun*, the country's leading family magazine. She has appeared twice on the *Today Show* and CBN with Pat Robertson. Beery's business has been featured in the *New York Times* and *Entrepreneur* magazine, as well as dozens of other local and national publications. She has worked closely with Get Moving, Cookies for Kids Cancer, Rachael Ray's Yum-o! Organization, and No Kids Hungry. Barbara is the author of 12 books, having sold more than 500,000 copies. She resides in Austin, Texas.

ABOUT FOODIE KIDS

Foodie Kids is the largest and most unique kids culinary center in the country. It includes a cooking school, retail store, and The Makery®, a drop-in make-your-own snack counter. The center started as a series of cooking classes in Barbara's home kitchen twenty-five years ago. Through the years, the small cooking school grew into an operation that was no longer manageable to operate from her home. With years of hard work, the small cottage business turned into a retail culinary destination for kids and families to celebrate birthdays, take cooking classes, host field trips, and enjoy summer cooking camps. For more information, visit www.foodie-kids.com.

ABOUT FAMILIUS

Familius is place where parents are celebrated, not compared. Where heart is at the center of our families, and family at the center of our homes. Where boo-boos are still kissed, cake beaters are still licked, and mistakes are still okay. Welcome to a place where books—and family—are beautiful. Familius: a book publisher dedicated to helping families be happy.